In koto chords

HAIKU By

MIHAELA BABUSANU

ISBN: 978-81-19228-49-2
Cover : Spring Art - Fine Art America-https://ro.pinterest.com

First Edition: 2023
Rs. 200/-

Cyberwit.net
HIG 45 Kaushambi Kunj, Kalindipuram
Allahabad - 211011 (U.P.) India
http://www.cyberwit.net
Tel: +(91) 9415091004
E-mail: info@cyberwit.net

1.

hurried passers-by-
those vows of eternal love
suddenly worthless

2.

evening on the hill-
alphorn ringing mournfully
over the village

3.

a warming spring breeze-
while the first snowdrop rises
someone called me mom

4.

day of separation-
sudden a cold autumn rain
whipping hard her face

5.

my first haiku book-
even the Fuji Mountain
it fits on pages

6.

november full moon -
we meet again in a dream
for the umpteenth time

7.

reunion after years
under her kimono's folds
hidden all his sins

8.

commemoration-
mother's and father's graves
just snow keeps them warm

9.

admiring bonsai-
with a ever greater goals
petite woman one

10.

a yellowed album-
fixing me from a picture
a girl with a doll

11

the end of winter-
in the painting of the girl
a cherry blossom

12.

a strong gust of wind-
torn away from an album
a picture with mom

9.

admiring bonsai-
with a ever greater goals
petite woman one

10.

a yellowed album-
fixing me from a picture
a girl with a doll

11

the end of winter-
in the painting of the girl
a cherry blossom

12.

a strong gust of wind-
torn away from an album
a picture with mom

13.

on Dragobete's Day-
on some benches in the park
so many scribbled hearts

14.

almost the sunset-
in the maternity ward
first screaming of child

15.

the summer estates-
mom takes out from the oven
another cheese pie

16.

few intense glances-
suddenly the "Swallow's Dress"
sudden transparent

17.

two storks in a nest-
very clear those images
from the ultrasound

18.

autumn sunset-
bouquet of chrysanthemums
on my mother's grave

19.

on Halloween night -
my former love memories
doesn't stop haunting me

20.

end of vacation-
grandfather sitting on porch
tearful once again

21.

another full moon-
counting how many nights passed
since i waiting you

22.

together again-
with Jupiter in Pisces
autumn begins

23.

first day of autumn-

only in the girl's painting

a blooming snowdrop

24.

scary Halloween-

too much botox for this time

on his girlfriend lips

25.

Hallow memories
the smell of that baked pumpkin
in parents' courtyard

26.

remeeting to tea-
the steams of that Jasmine tea
as hot as ever

27.

around the fireplace-
tales told by the grandmother
sparking much questions

28.

reunion after years-
a "Forget-me-not" flower
rising on the path

29.

first snow of this year-
observing in the mirror
first strands of white hair

30.

the end of autumn-
more and more harder the slope
for the old woman

31.

so enigmatic-
just a Cucuteni crock
and so much to say

32.

Sunday to the church-
mother brings sunflowers oil
as a thank to God

33.

end of brumar-
no trace of smoke from chimney
at my parent's house

34.

old shepherd village -
going out into the streets
smoke from meat smokers

35.

the deserted house-

since nine years under cobwebs

the dad hunting boots

36.

sunflower season-

after four boys in a row

mother hugs first girl

37.

recent spring picture—
instead of the cuckoo's song
the sound of the shells

38.

separation day-
high above the mountain tops
a few crows circling

39.

rejoined after years-
her kimono with dragons
suits her just as well

40.

reminding first kiss-
one by one all the night stars
burning in his eyes

41.

the day of breakup-
aroused from almost nowhere
even an ice rain

42.

Children's Day from june
grandfather sudden wishes
a cotton candy

43.

reunion after years -
his perfume arriving first
from the parking lot

44.

a jasmine flower –
suddenly slipped in my mind
a few love poems

45.

seventeen april-
i wear kimono again
with cherry blossoms

46.

some jasmine flowers-
only your body odor
in competition

47.

few cherry blossoms-
waiting for the muse again
to write a haiku

48.

vivid memories-
in the album with us two
two pressed snowdrops too

49.

forester's widow-
no voice resounds in the house
only the birdsong

50.

after years apart-
our hearts in the same rhythm
with icicles drips

51.

a terrible frost-
your black eyes staring at me
sudden warming me

52.

a big Christmas tree-
the lights turn on in your eyes
when we meet again

53.

few pennies clanking-
lighting almost suddenly
eyes of the blind man

54.

cold winter evening-
grandma put me on a tray
a hot jasmine tea

55.

bullet wounded man-
those deep blue eyes of the nurse
hitting straight his heart

56.

dreaming of a prince-
suddenly from that old pond
a noisy male frog

57.

the final outcome-
the young woman convicted
waiting anxiously

58.

heady waterfall-
fragmentary memories
of my former love

59.

casting in progress-
posing so naturally
just a dragonfly

60

all boats on the shore-
failed far away on the sea
even my last hopes

61

toghether again-

over the greened peaks again

the sun shine again

62.

back into lockdown -

becoming blurred in my mind

cherry blossom scent

63.

first fresh snow this year-
so feverishly waiting
to see your footprints

64.

on Thanksgiving Day-
the fish soup warming his hands
to the old beggar

65.

to the meeting place-
trapped just like in a whirlwind
our hearts and the leaves

66.

two mature lovers
sudden expelled by the storm-
just a lightning kiss

67

a lightning fast kiss-
sudden a huge avalanche
sparked out of nowhere

68

frosty vineyard-
those vacation memories
sweeter than the stum

69.

neither me nor him-
today just a hard sadness
swinging in the swing

70.

towards the sunset-
harder and harder to climb
all the steps of life

71.

in our old walnut-
a merry flock of starlings
the nuts on the ground

72.

a chrysanthemum-
under of my lover steps
a hard broken heart

73.

the house in ruins-
as vigorous as ever
a honeysuckle

74.

carving a cradle-
a stork in a magnolia
full of new fresh buds

75.

a funeral suite-
rolled suddenly in the road
some bitter cherries

www.ingramcontent.com/pod-product-compliance
Lightning Source LLC
LaVergne TN
LVHW040929150826
845672LV00007B/2267

* 9 7 8 8 1 1 9 2 2 8 4 9 2 *